The Hollywood Walk of Shame

The **HOLLY**

*The Most Outrageously Funny Moments
in Show Business History*

WOOD
Walk of Shame.

Bruce Nash and Allan Zullo

Compiled by Martha Moffett

Andrews and McMeel ✳ *A Universal Press Syndicate Company* ✳ Kansas City

Designed by Rick Cusick

Library of Congress Cataloging-in-Publication Data

Nash, Bruce M.
    The Hollywood walk of shame : the most outrageously
funny moments in show business history / Bruce Nash and
Allan Zullo ; compiled by Martha Moffett.
      p.   cm.
   ISBN 0-8362-8035-0 : $6.95
   1. Motion pictures—United States—Humor. 2. Television
broadcasting—United States—Humor. 3. Motion picture industry—
United States—Anecdotes. 4. Television broadcasting—United
States—Anecdotes. 5. Entertainers—United States—Anecdotes.
I. Zullo, Allan. II. Moffett, Martha L. III. Title.
PN1994.9.N37   1993
791,43'0973—dc20   93-25432
                                                    CIP

ATTENTION: SCHOOLS AND BUSINESSES
Andrews and McMeel books are available at quantity discounts with bulk purchase
for educational, business, or sales promotional use. For information, please write to:
Special Sales Department, Andrews and McMeel, 4900 Main Street, Kansas City, Missouri 64112.

To my friend Brad Turell, whose star will one day shine brightly
on the Hollywood Walk of Fame.

—Bruce Nash

To Ray and Jodi Benson, may they shine on the silver screen
with the dazzle they've displayed on the Great White Way.

—Allan Zullo

Contents

Ever since 1984, we have been compiling the most embarrassing and zany moments in sports history in our best-selling Sports Hall of Shame book series. But now we've turned our sights from the playing fields of sports to the soundstages of Hollywood, searching for the funniest foul-ups and goofiest gaffes of our all-time favorite show biz stars.

Let's face it. Everyone makes mistakes—even Tinseltown's most famous movie and TV personalities. And when show business celebrities screw up, they deserve some special recognition for their blunders. If the big names in the entertainment world can receive stars on the Hollywood Walk of Fame for their achievements, then they should receive stars on *The Hollywood Walk of Shame* for their goof-ups.

This book is a lighthearted tribute to the blunderful moments experienced by such acting legends as Gregory Peck, Jimmy Stewart, and Marilyn Monroe, as well as today's hottest stars such as Tom Cruise, Ted Danson, and Michelle Pfeiffer. From the days of the silent movies to television's newest sitcom, Hollywood has been teeming with such ignoble incidents and hilarious happenings as:

Julia Roberts ordering an entire movie crew to strip down to their underwear because she had to film a scene in her undershirt and panties.

Johnny Carson, with an off-the-cuff remark, unwittingly starting a nationwide buying panic for toilet paper.

Ronald Reagan nearly being choked to death by his simian co-star—the chimp that appeared with him in the 1951 movie *Bedtime for Bonzo*.

Paul Newman cutting the desk of his director in half with a chain saw.

We hope you'll enjoy this offbeat chronicle of the wacky side of Hollywood. Meanwhile, we will continue to compile the most embarrassing and funny moments in show biz history.

Bombs Away!
Atrocious Movie and TV Flops

Lost Cos

Leonard Part 6 was such a bomb that even before it was released, the film's star-producer Bill Cosby went to some shocking extremes to defuse it—he tried to prevent people from seeing the movie!

First, the Cos offered to buy the $20 million picture from Columbia to take it out of distribution. When that failed, he took the unusual tactic of actually telling the public to stay away from his very own film.

In this 1987 spy spoof—which Cosby himself helped write—Cosby plays the title character, a secret agent who tries to thwart a villainess plotting to take over the world by using a special formula that turns animals into killers. Unfortunately, advance screenings showed, the film was neither funny nor interesting. Apparently, Cosby realized it, too.

So he did something no major star had ever done before—publicly asking fans not to see his movie. "I've enjoyed a lot of success through the years," Cosby told the press at the time. "But I'm not too big to admit when I've made a bomb . . . and *Leonard* is a bomb. That's why I tried to buy back the rights to the movie. The only trouble is, I'm not *that* wealthy. But I don't want to shortchange my loyal fans. So if they pay to see it, they can't say I didn't warn them."

Cosby's warning worked. Fans stayed away by the millions and the movie flopped big time.

Said the *1988 Motion Picture Annual*: "The narrator explains at the beginning of the film that the first five of Leonard's adventures couldn't be revealed in the interest of national security. The movie-going public would have been better served had Leonard's most recent adventure also been kept under lock and key."

Loser by a Knockout—Matilda!

A movie about a boxing kangaroo wound up such a cinema turkey that the only way some theaters could sell tickets was to bill it as the year's worst movie!

In 1978, Al Ruddy produced *Matilda*, a film about a kangaroo that battles its way to a boxing championship. The movie got kayoed because of a lousy script, bad acting, and a godawful kangaroo. Rather than use a trained animal, Ruddy spent $30,000 on a kangaroo suit that looked like a homemade trick-or-treat costume and stuck actor Gary Morgan inside.

Spirits were high during the making of the film. Ruddy cut deals with major corporations for product tie-ins and cross-promotions. McDonald's planned to put Matilda's face in TV spots, print ads, posters, and giveaways, and introduce a line of Matilda sundaes. The promotional campaign was so gigantic that *Variety* predicted, "By the end of summer, no living American should be unaware that Matilda is a boxing kangaroo."

The truth is, by the end of summer, there were hardly any living Americans who had seen—or even wanted to see—the movie. That's because the reviews were unanimous in labeling *Matilda* a big-time loser. Faster than the kangaroo could throw a punch, every corporate promotional deal was canceled.

Because of the overwhelmingly bad reviews, on the day the film opened at a San Francisco movie house, not a single patron showed up. But the theater owner decided to turn this lemon into lemonade with a clever promotion that other theaters soon tried.

Knowing he had to carry this bomb for a few more days, he went out and changed the marquee. Using the words of a local reviewer, the marquee now read, "WORST MOVIE OF THE YEAR" and included the name of the critic. Business picked up considerably because people were curious enough to pay a few bucks just to see what could make a movie so terrible.

They found out.

Viva La Bomba!

One of the strangest flops in film history was a documentary of the Mexican revolution.

Incredibly, legendary Mexican rebel Pancho Villa turned his country's bloody upheaval into the only war ever fought for the movie cameras. In 1914, he sold the exclusive film rights of his battles to the Mutual Film Company for $25,000 plus a percentage of the profits. The footage of his skirmishes was edited into the movie *The Life of Villa.*

But what was so bizarre about the film was how it was made. Villa actually ordered his soldiers to fight only in daylight—because the cameras couldn't film the action at night! The rebel engaged in bitter arguments with his top lieutenants who were pushing for night attacks, but he stood firm on his agreement with the studio to fight only during the day.

Villa seemed more intent on making a good movie than on winning the revolution. Often, while Villa and his men were plotting their strategy, the movie producer objected because the planned battles wouldn't make good footage. Each time, Villa ordered the plans changed for the sake of better location and action shots.

Once, when Villa's forces surrounded a government stronghold, he held off the final attack for two hours until a camera could get into the correct position.

Another time, when Villa's men were waiting to ambush government troops, the producer complained that he wouldn't get any decent camera shots because the rebels' machine guns had a greater range than his camera. So Villa agreed to hold fire until the enemy soldiers were within camera range. He then ordered his troops to shoot—but only after the producer had given him the OK!

When *The Life of Villa* was finished, the Mexican rebel saw it and loved it. Unfortunately, hardly anyone north of the border did. The movie was sent south and was never seen again.

Give 'em the (Heaven's) Gate

No movie was a bigger bomb than *Heaven's Gate*.

The 1980 epic—about the conflict between immigrant settlers and ruthless empire-builders in nineteenth-century Wyoming—made cinema history by ending up an astounding $100 million in the red!

The blame for the debacle fell squarely on the shoulders of writer-director Michael Cimino. If they gave Oscars for squandering money, wasting time, and obsessing over retakes, Cimino would win all three dubious awards unanimously.

Production was initially budgeted at $7.8 million. Cimino went over that figure by $36 million. The studio, United Artists, had an inkling of trouble when, after the first six days of shooting, Cimino was five days behind schedule.

But it was the director's outrageous spending habits that caused the biggest concern for the studio.

He filmed much of the movie in Glacier National Park and the nearby town of Kalispell, Montana. Despite the magnificent vistas, Cimino brought in tons of dirt, covered acres of unspoiled grasslands with brown and yellow paint, and hauled in hundreds of trees.

Cimino insisted that hundreds of film technicians on location be on call eighteen hours a day, seven days a week. That proved to be extremely expensive. Most of the technicians worked less than ten hours a day, but because of union rules, Cimino had to pay his crew for twenty-four-hour shifts at triple time. As a result, technicians who normally worked for $1,000 a week were getting $5,000 a week for six months.

Then there was the street scene flap. After an entire set of the main street of a western town was built to his exact specifications, Cimino felt the buildings made the street look too narrow. So he ordered the buildings on both sides of the street torn down and moved back three feet each. When someone suggested it would be easier and cheaper to keep one side up and simply shift the other one back six feet, Cimino refused. So both sides of the completed street set were torn down and reconstructed, at a cost of $550,000.

Cimino drove the cast nuts with his endless retakes. He ordered a whopping fifty-three  retakes of a scene in which actor Kris Kristofferson whips some settlers. Another scene that called for an actor to moon a crowd of immigrants was reshot thirty times, prompting one cameraman to mutter, "How many different ways can a guy drop his pants?"

In September, 1979, when he was six months behind schedule, Cimino threw a party on location to celebrate the exposure of his one-millionth foot of film—a record for a single movie. (Most directors don't shoot over 100,000 feet.)

After millions of dollars in cost overruns and delays, the filming was finally completed. Then Cimino spent another six months editing it down to a "bare bones" three hours, thirty-nine minutes. United Artists spent nearly $2 million to hype the film prior to its first screening—mostly for reporters and critics—in November, 1980.

The critics savaged the film: "*Heaven's Gate* is something quite rare in movies these days —an unqualified disaster," said the *New York Times*. Said another critic: "Cimino's spectacle is missing just one thing—a story." The reviews were so overwhelmingly bad that the much-publicized premiere slated for the following week was postponed so Cimino could re-edit the debacle.

By now, United Artists bigwigs were in a panic. Heads were rolling as the press reported the film would have to gross $140 million just to break even. One studio source, trying desperately to look on the bright side, told *The Wall Street Journal*, "We know some people will go to see the picture simply to say, 'I told you it was a bomb!'"

In April, 1981, *Heaven's Gate* made its official world premiere in Hollywood. When the credits rolled at the end, the audience booed.

This scene was played out pretty much the same throughout the country in hundreds of theaters—that is, where there was much of an audience. At the end of the first week, the movie had grossed a paltry $1.3 million. According to the *Los Angeles Times,* that averaged out to just over $500 a night for each theater, "which will barely pay for film cans used to transport prints of *Heaven's Gate.*"

Since its opening, the movie has become Hollywood's most infamous bomb. With the additional editing, advertising, distribution, and other charges, the studio lost at least $100 million on Cimino's film folly.

So who did Cimino blame for the fiasco? The moviegoing public! He claimed Americans weren't interested in seeing a beautiful film that was a testament to his craftsmanship

17

and individuality. Lamented Cimino, "I think we are gradually in the process of losing the value we placed on those qualities."

The truth is, the only value that movie patrons were losing was the cost of a ticket to *Heaven's Gate*.

No Laughing Matter

Ishtar was the *Heaven's Gate* of movie comedies.

In this 1987 buddy-buddy film, Warren Beatty and Dustin Hoffman play two untalented singer-songwriters who get involved with international intrigue in North Africa. In a bizarre bit of casting, Hoffman plays the slick lover boy and Beatty the nerd sidekick. And they sing all or part of the movie's twenty-six songs slightly off-key.

It may have been billed as a funny picture, but no one—not the audiences, the critics, or the studio bosses—was laughing. From a financial standpoint, this was no comedy; this was a disaster film. Columbia bean counters estimated that the movie would have to gross $100 million just to recoup the initial investment. By the end of 1992, the film had taken in less than $13 million.

At a time when the average Hollywood movie cost $17 million, *Ishtar* cost $13 million before a single foot of film was shot. That's because Beatty and Hoffman each pocketed $5.5 million for their acting fees, Elaine May received $1.5 million as writer-director, and Beatty earned another $500,000 as producer.

With a production budget of $40 million, *Ishtar* was the most expensive comedy ever made. "What is most distressing about the size of the budget is that the money is not on the screen," wrote a critic for the *1988 Motion Picture Annual*. "Somehow, May managed to spend $40 million on two guys singing, a bunch of robed extras, a blind camel, and some sand dunes."

May, who filmed on location in the desert of Morocco, lived up to her reputation for wasteful shooting methods. Because she insisted on numerous retakes, May shot 500,000 feet of film (five times the average) and used only about 10,000 feet.

Unfortunately, the script wasn't a rib-tickler and, try as they might, the two big-name stars couldn't save it. They had a feeling this overpriced comedy would bomb. In an interview in *People* magazine prior to the film's release, Hoffman joked that *Ishtar* was "a chance for the audience to come and see the end of two careers."

Although Hoffman and Beatty survived the bomb, their fears that the movie would flop were realized. Reviewers tore it apart, echoing the *Hollywood Reporter*, which called it "colossally dunderheaded." Said *People* magazine: "Near the end, lying exhausted after a sandstorm, Beatty and Hoffman find themselves perused by two hungry vultures. 'We're not dead. We're just resting,' the boys wail. Maybe. Audiences, enduring the stupor of *Ishtar*, are likely to side with the vultures."

Attack Dogs

Movies whose title starts with the word "Attack" usually send audiences in retreat because these films are such dogs. For example:

Attack of the Crab Monsters (1957)—People are trapped on a shrinking island by intelligent, brain-eating, giant crabs.

Attack of the 50 Ft. Woman (1958)—A nasty, shrill wife grows to mammoth proportions after an alien encounter and then harasses her philandering husband.

Attack of the Puppet People (1958)—A mad scientist shrinks people and then uses them for evil.

Attack of the Giant Leeches (1959)—Huge leeches in a southern swamp suck the blood out of terrified locals.

Attack of the Mayan Mummy (1963)—A scientist gets his patient to revert to a former life and reveal the site of an ancient tomb; the movie uses footage from old Mexican horror films.

The Squawk Over the Hawk

Of all the action movies ever made, none was as costly a flop as *Hudson Hawk*.

Tri Star Pictures took an estimated $60 million bath on this 1991 bomb—a labor of love for its writer-star Bruce Willis. He spent twelve years developing the story idea for this widely condemned offbeat adventure about a smirking cat burglar's attempt to retrieve a part for a machine Leonardo da Vinci once used to turn lead into gold. "Could Tri Star ever use that machine now!" said the *New York Times*.

Millions of dollars were squandered on dozens of script rewrites, snail-paced filming, and cost overruns in Hungary, Italy, and England. The producers spent a bundle renting the Brooklyn Bridge for a week to film Willis careening across the span in a gurney for barely a minute of onscreen footage.

Not since *Heaven's Gate* had a major motion picture incurred such universal censure from the critics and public alike. Words like "brainless," "witless," "gutless," and "tasteless" kept cropping up in reviews. *People* magazine put it in simple, blunt language: "This is the movie playing all the time on every screen of every theater in hell. . . . This, in short, is a chance to see the most hateful movie of all time."

Sour Notes

The 1975 musical *At Long Last Love* was so bad that the guy who produced and directed this bomb took out a full-page ad to apologize!

For whatever reason, Peter Bogdanovich chose as his singing and dancing stars Cybill Shepherd and Burt Reynolds, who were the first to admit they could neither sing nor dance—and proved it on the screen. The couple

were no Fred Astaire and Ginger Rogers. They were, according to the *New York Times*, actors "who have between them four left feet."

That was bad enough. Even worse was Bogdanovich's insistence that all the musical numbers—there were sixteen Cole Porter tunes—be recorded live, so there was no chance the off-key stars could be saved by dubbing real singers' voices.

When the movie turned into a multimillion-dollar musical bomb, a chastened Bogdanovich felt compelled to make a public apology. He took out a full-page ad in *The Hollywood Reporter* and admitted that the film "was to prove the perhaps lame-brained theory of the director that musicals ought to be done entirely live."

TV Turkeys

The television landscape has been pockmarked with an incredible number of series that bombed, including some that didn't last a month—or even a week. Among some of the biggest flops:

"Apple Pie" (1978). This sitcom starred Rue McClanahan (later of "Golden Girls" fame) as a lonely hairdresser who recruits a "family" through the want ads and gets a con-man husband, tap-dancing daughter, and a son who wants to fly like a bird. The show was canceled after just two episodes.

"B.A.D. Cats" (1980). This was a drama about two race-drivers-turned-cops who chase the bad guys using souped-up police cars. The series, which lasted one month, was so bad that producer Everett Chambers confided to reporters, "I'm not putting this as one of my credits."

"Flatbush" (1979). The exploits of five Italian high school graduates in Brooklyn were featured in this critically creamed series. The ethnic stereotypes so offended the real-life Brooklyn borough president that he publicly demanded the series be taken off the air before it gave the city a bad name. CBS agreed, and trashed the show after only three episodes.

"No Soap, Radio" (1982). Like the title itself, this comedy, starring Steve Guttenberg, simply didn't make much sense to viewers. The action took place in a strange hotel where residents chased a man-eating chair, a little old lady was attacked by a submarine, a gunfighter raged because his opponent overslept, and a sci-fi flick on the hotel TV was showing *The Day Everyone's Name Became Al.* In real life, the network canned the series after a month.

"Once a Hero" (1987). In this fantasy-adventure, a cartoon superhero crossed into the real world because he feared his comic strip was about to get canceled. What did get canceled was this show, after only three episodes.

"Turn-On" (1969). This fast-paced comedy, billed as the second coming of "Laugh-In," lasted exactly one show because of widespread condemnation for its sexual innuendo. For example, in one skit, a beautiful, sexy woman is about to be executed by a firing squad. Instead of asking her if she had a last request, the leering squad leader suggestively tells her, "I know this may seem a little unusual, miss, but in this case the firing squad has one last request." The show contained so many sexual double entendres that the sponsor and network affiliates refused to carry it after the first telecast and it was immediately canceled.

Picture Imperfect

Jackie Gleason once hosted a TV game show that was so awful it was canned after exactly one telecast. Not only that, but the following week, The Great One apologized for the bomb in front of a nationwide audience!

The fiasco, which aired on January 20, 1961, on CBS, was called "You're in the Picture." Four celebrity panelists noted for their humor—Keenan Wynn, Pat Carroll, Jan Sterling, and Arthur Treacher —had to stick their heads and hands through an oversized carnival cutout without knowing what the picture represented. The panelists then tried to guess what the cutout was by asking questions of Gleason, who was the host of the show. When they had successfully identified the picture, they would start over with a new cutout.

Gleason's wit was supposed to add to the humor of the show, which was played primarily for laughs. But the concept was so lame and the jokes were so strained that the network biggies and Gleason himself decided to pull the plug after just one telecast.

Viewers who tuned in the following week were astonished to see Gleason sitting in an armchair on an otherwise bare stage. In a first for television, the chagrined host spent the entire half hour apologizing to the country for the TV disaster.

"I apologize for insulting your intelligence," Gleason told viewers. "From now on, I promise to stick to comedy."

For the remainder of the season, Gleason filled the time slot by interviewing a different celebrity each week in a talk show called "The Jackie Gleason Show."

It Was a Very Bad Year

Nancy Walker and Pat Morita gained a dubious distinction during the 1976–1977 TV season. They each starred in two comedy series that bombed.

"The Nancy Walker Show" and Morita's series, "Mr. T and Tina," both debuted on ABC in September, 1976. His show—about a Japanese inventor and his nutty American housekeeper—

was canceled in October after only one month. Walker's series—in which she starred as a talent agent married to a Navy man—lasted until December.

Not to be denied, the network brought the two stars together in a new replacement series in February called "Blansky's Beauties." It was a comedy in which Walker was a den mother to a bevy of Las Vegas showgirls and Morita played the owner of a coffee shop. However, like both their earlier series, this one failed, too, and was canceled three months later.

It's a Blunderful Life

Zany Show Biz Bloopers

Monty Hall's Breast Blooper of All Time

Of the thousands of "Let's Make a Deal" shows that Monty Hall hosted, he was bound to commit some bloopers. But there was one gaffe that stood out above the rest.

It happened during the end of a show when Hall went into the audience and offered people money if they had certain objects in their possession.

"I saw a woman who was holding a baby doll and she was pretending to feed it with a bottle," Hall recalled. "It was part of a costume she was wearing. I walked up, took the baby bottle from her, and said, 'Show me another nipple and I'll give you $200.'

"Naturally, the place fell apart. It took me a split second to realize what I'd said. What I'd meant was I wanted to see another rubber nipple like she had on the baby bottle. The audience was hysterical with laughter—and I made it even worse by saying, 'I didn't mean that.' I should have kept my mouth shut, because if there was anybody in the audience who had missed the double meaning, they sure got it then."

The laughter continued for another thirty seconds, right up until the show went off the air, without the chagrined Hall ever able to say another word.

Heeeere's Johnny's Best Bloopers

Slipping up on TV can be either terribly embarrassing or absolutely hilarious—depending on which side of the camera you're on. Some of the funniest bloopers of all time occurred on "The Tonight Show Starring Johnny Carson." For example:

✶ Introducing his guests one evening, Johnny Carson said, "And on our show tonight, we have five Miss America contestants and also some dogs . . ." The audience burst out laughing. "I mean real dogs . . ." The laughter got even louder. "Come on, now, you know I mean dogs that bark!"

✶ While describing a party she had thrown, ditzy blonde Carol Wayne said, "I had my first big affair. I had forty people." Another time, telling about a beer commercial she had done, Wayne said, "I never knew those beer people were so fussy. If your can isn't turned just the right way, they let you know." After the audience stopped laughing, she added, "And they have special stuff they spray on your can to make it look wet and delicious."

✶ While interviewing Frank and Helen Beardsley, a married couple with twenty children, Carson asked, "How do you manage, having twenty children?" Mrs. Beardsley replied, "I am doing what I enjoy most. I guess I was just made for it."

✶ On a pre-Christmas program, Carson told his audience, "I'm going to read some letters from legitimate children." When the audience roared, he said, "Come on, you know what I mean—legitimate letters from children."

✻ While introducing a new sponsor, Carson held up a can of paint and was interrupted by guest Carol Channing who said she also used the product. "You see," Carson told his audience, "an ordinary lady we picked up off the street." After the audience burst out laughing, an embarrassed Carson said, "I don't mean *that* kind of lady."

✻ Ed Ames, who played an Indian on the TV series "Daniel Boone," demonstrated his tomahawk-throwing prowess on a wooden silhouette of a human figure. But instead of hitting the heart or the head, the blade buried itself in the most private part of the anatomy. The blunder got the biggest, longest laugh in the show's history.

Carson's Toilet Paper Caper

With one off-the-cuff remark, Johnny Carson unwittingly started a nationwide buying panic for toilet paper!

In 1973, during a monologue on one of his shows, Carson said, "Have you heard the latest? I'm not kidding. I saw it in the paper. There's a shortage of toilet paper."

Actually, what he read was that someone had started a *rumor* about a TP shortage. But for millions of viewers—and shoppers—Carson triggered "what may go down in history as one of the nation's most unusual crises," according to the *New York Times*. "This was a phenomenon that saw millions of Americans strip every roll of bathroom tissue from thousands of grocery shelves."

Finally, after a week or two of a toilet paper buying binge across the country, the run on the precious commodity subsided.

Can We Talk?

On her talk show, Joan Rivers let her fingers do a little too much walking and her mouth a little too much talking when she tried to telephone Victoria Principal.

In 1986, Rivers had "Dallas" star Ken (Cliff Barnes) Kercheval on her program, "The Late Show Starring Joan Rivers," when she decided to telephone Principal, who played Pamela Barnes Ewing on the hit series. Getting a busy signal, Rivers tried phoning her between each guest spot.

When that failed, Rivers called the operator, announced that she was a doctor, and asked to be put through. But in the process, Rivers did the unthinkable. She laughingly repeated Principal's phone number loud enough for her nationwide TV audience to hear.

Sure enough, hundreds of people tried to call Principal, who was forced to take her phone off the hook. In fact, there were so many calls that the circuits jammed and the phone company had to change her number the very next day.

The Whole Tooth and Nothing But the Tooth

While belting out a song in a Broadway musical, Angela Lansbury had to grin and bear it—because her tooth flew out of her mouth and narrowly missed hitting acting legend Laurence Olivier!

Angela, well-known for her role as Jessica Fletcher in the hit TV series "Murder, She Wrote," was starring on the Great White Way in the musical *Sweeney Todd* at the Uris Theater in

1979. She played the bawdy pie-shop owner, Mrs. Lovett, to rave reviews. In fact, it was because of Lansbury's stunning performance that Olivier decided to see the show. He was given the best seat in the house—front row, center.

When Angela learned that the great Olivier was in the theater, she was determined to make her performance an unforgettable one. And she did—but not in the way she had intended.

During the first act, Angela was in the middle of a song when she felt a temporary front tooth loosen. Before she could do anything about it, the tooth gave way and flew out of her mouth and over the footlights.

"To my great surprise and horror, my tooth barely missed Larry, who was sitting down front!" Lansbury recalled. "For one terrible moment, time stood still. There I was with a gap in my mouth where the tooth once was. I'd never been so embarrassed in all my life.

"For the rest of the song, I had to hide the gap and sing through the side of my mouth. It was simply awful.

"They say that in the face of such mishaps, one should 'grin and bear it.' But at the time, grinning wasn't the appropriate thing to do.

"I don't think Larry cared too much for the show. However, he did pay me a lovely compliment. Noticing something I did on stage, he said, 'You're one of the few actresses who can bend her hand backward on her wrist.'

"That was the extent of his critique of *Sweeney Todd*! He never mentioned that he almost got hit with my tooth."

The Naked and the Red

Entertainer Red Buttons turned as crimson as his first name after accidentally getting stripped naked during a live nationwide telecast.

In the early 1950s, Buttons was a guest on "The Milton Berle Show." For a sketch, Berle played a doctor trying to treat a patient, portrayed by Buttons, who was too shy to take off his clothes.

Buttons was wearing a special trick suit made in such a way that the coat, shirt, and pants were one piece and could be pulled off him with one yank on the shirt collar.

"When my character refused to get undressed, Milton was supposed to grab my shirt front and rip the entire thing off—and I'd be left standing there in old-fashioned, knee-to-neck one-piece underwear," Buttons recalled. "That was the laugh.

"Well, Milton reached for my shirt and by mistake grabbed me under the collar. And when he yanked at my breakaway suit, everything came off—including my underwear! We were on live television. And there I stood—nude in front of a studio audience and all the people watching at home.

"When I realized what had happened, I got right behind Milton, who was as shocked as I was, but who had the presence of mind to announce the next act and have the curtain closed.

"I turned as red as my hair from embarrassment!"

A Rip-Roaring Song

Country and western singer Johnny Cash revealed more about himself than he cared to during a dinner honoring former First Lady Mamie Eisenhower.

In 1962, some of the biggest names in Hollywood were entertaining at a lavish black-tie affair in Mamie's honor at the Waldorf Astoria Hotel in New York. Mamie sat enthralled in the front row as the stars tried to outshine each other. When it was Cash's turn to sing, he was suffering a bad case of the jitters.

"I hit the first lick on my guitar and I was so nervous that I dropped my pick," Cash recalled. But what minor embarrassment he felt then was nothing compared with the mortification he experienced seconds later. When Cash bent down to retrieve his pick, his right pants leg ripped open all the way from his knee to his crotch!

"I glanced over at Mamie Eisenhower and her face had turned bright red," Cash recalled. "She was trying to keep back a smile while I was still trying to get that pick off the floor. And since that was the only pick I had, I just had to keep trying to get it. It seemed like an eternity."

Cash could hear muffled giggles from the audience as he finally managed to grab his pick, straighten up, and sing. "When I finished, I was so upset I wasn't even able to smile or bow to the audience," he recalled. "I ran offstage and took the elevator straight up to my hotel suite. That was my most embarrassing moment."

You Won't Have Rich Little to Kick Around Anymore

Comic impressionist Rich Little felt like a big fool when he tried to make President Richard Nixon laugh—and failed.

In 1970, Little and other Hollywood celebrities were invited to the president's San Clemente, California, home for a party. Nixon was standing outside by the pool with his guests when Debbie Reynolds announced that Little was going to do his impression of the chief executive.

"Mr. Nixon turned around and faced me," recalled Little. "I finally wound up saying something inane in his voice like, 'Let me make this perfectly clear. I think this is a marvelous party. Make no mistake about that.' And I finished by giving the Nixon V-for-victory sign.

"There was dead silence when I finished. There was no laughing or clapping, just silence. Mr. Nixon simply stared at me. It became painfully obvious to me that he didn't know who I was or what I was doing.

"Then the president turned to Mrs. Nixon and whispered, 'Why is that man talking in that strange voice?' I can't remember ever being so embarrassed."

Dead Wrong

During a press conference at the 1990 Deauville Film Festival in France, TV miniseries king Richard Chamberlain was asked which French film director he would most like to work with in the future. "François Truffaut," said Chamberlain without hesitation.

After an awkward moment of silence, a French reporter informed the actor that Truffaut had been dead for nearly six years. "I didn't know," confessed the chagrined actor.

Hitting the Wrong Note

During a nightclub performance, singer Lou Rawls read aloud a note from a waitress—and then wished he had zipped his lips.

Rawls was singing at a Fort Lauderdale night spot in 1969, and because it was a casual atmosphere, he performed in a shirt and slacks instead of the formal attire he usually wore on stage. After he had finished a song, one of the waitresses walked up and handed him a note.

"I figured it was just a request for a certain song, so I laid it down on top of the piano without looking at it and kept on singing," Rawls recalled. "A few minutes later, I picked up the note. I'd always read requests out loud for the audiences to hear. So I started reading the note aloud into the microphone: 'Dear Lou. We know you don't know this, but all the waitresses are standing in the back really breaking up—because your fly is open!'

"I stood there for a moment. I didn't do a quick about-face. I really didn't do anything except freeze and offer a goofy grin." Then he zipped up his fly to the roar of the audience and launched into his next song.

"Ever since then," he said, "I quickly scan any note from the audience before I read it out loud."

A Christmas Carol

During the eleven-year run of "The Carol Burnett Show," the comedienne would answer impromptu questions from the audience at the beginning of each show. Only once was Burnett stumped.

"It was August, but we were taping our Christmas show, so in the warm-up I warned the audience not to be surprised by all the carols and snowflakes," Burnett recalled.

When the taping began, she turned to the audience and began answering questions with her usually witty quips. But there was one question which left her speechless. Recounted Burnett, "A man stood up and asked me what I got for Christmas."

Behind the Scenes

Hilarious Happenings that Audiences Didn't See

Reality Check

Woody Harrelson and Kevin Costner practiced so hard for their starring roles in their respective sports-themed movies *White Men Can't Jump* and *Bull Durham* that they began to believe they actually were as good as pro athletes.

So Ron Shelton, who directed both films, decided to teach the two stars a lesson in humility—and reality.

Before the 1992 shooting of *White Men Can't Jump*, a comedy about a pair of hard court basketball hustlers, Harrelson and co-star Wesley Snipes survived a four-week basketball boot camp and spent countless hours playing hoops until they looked and played like veteran playground warriors. They were swift dribblers, dead-eye shooters, and clever passers. The problem was, said Shelton, that Harrelson began to think he was a great player. So he set the actor up for a little reality check.

One scene called for Harrelson to go one-on-one with Freeman Williams, a former NBA sharpshooter of the early 1980s who was portraying a playground rival. Williams was supposed to go easy on the star.

But back behind the cameras, Shelton turned to basketball consultant Rob Ryder and said, "I think we should let Freeman have a go at Woody."

"Let him loose?" Ryder asked.

"Yeah," Shelton said with a grin. "Humiliate him." The director then walked over to Williams and said, "Freeman, take it to the hole every chance you get." In other words, drive to the basket against Harrelson.

When the cameras started to roll, Williams gave Harrelson an icy stare, then faked right, went left, and rocketed to the basket and dunked it while a befuddled Harrelson helplessly watched. Again and again, Williams drove left, right, and over his now-flustered opponent until Shelton shouted, "Hey, Woody. Welcome to the real world."

KEVIN COSTNER

Four years earlier, in 1988, Shelton felt the need to teach Costner a similar lesson during the shooting of *Bull Durham*, a funny, sassy film about minor league baseball. Costner, who played ball in college, proudly swatted several home runs during batting practice. "He started to get a little cocky," recalled Shelton, who spent five years in the minor leagues before turning to a movie career.

Costner was making some comments about how he could have made it to the big leagues if he had tried. So Shelton challenged Costner to hit ninety-mile-an-hour major league fastballs. The actor dug his feet into the dirt of the batter's box and confidently waited for the first pitch.

The next thing he knew, he was eating dust, having hit the ground to avoid a brushback pitch. After a few more "dusters" and some curveballs and fastballs, Costner was lucky if he could just foul off a pitch.

"Sometimes we threw a few fastballs close to his head," Shelton said. "Kevin got the message. He'd go, 'Oh, I get it. That's the real thing.'"

Little Squirt

The TV show "Evening Shade" became "Evening *Sprayed*" when Burt Reynolds was bathing his new TV baby Emily in the kitchen sink during a scene in 1990.

Suddenly, the infant answered nature's call right in Burt's face! Reynolds just grinned and hurried off to change shirts as the studio audience roared with laughter.

Only then did the audience realize that Emily was really a he—actually, two he's. During the audition for the part of his baby daughter, Reynolds chose the twin boys because he thought they were the cutest babies. The boys take turns playing Emily.

Julia Roberts's Brief Encounter

During the shooting of the 1991 thriller *Sleeping with the Enemy*, Julia Roberts devised a nutty way to speed up the filming of a scene—she ordered the entire crew to strip down to their underwear!

On a cold night along the South Carolina seashore, Julia was soaking wet, shivering, and clad in an undershirt and panties. The scene called for her to emerge from the ocean and run into her beach house in her skivvies. That's when the actress decided that if she had to run around half-naked in her undies, so would everyone else.

"I think we need a little group support here," she told the crew. "So drop your drawers. If you're not going to take your pants off, you can't stay in the house for the filming."

At first, the crew laughed nervously. But then they fell silent when they realized she meant it. Director Joe Ruben reluctantly agreed with his star, and was the first to strip to his shorts. About half the crew bailed out, but the rest followed Julia's orders.

She then grabbed her camera and gleefully took pictures of them—the lighting men crouched in the corner in their shorts; the crew member who wasn't wearing any underwear and had to wrap a towel around his waist; and the shy camera assistant who shocked everyone by wearing pink boxer shorts emblazoned with words like "bam," "whap," and "zap."

Julia later told reporters, "We all had a laugh and the night went a lot faster—because anybody working in his underwear wants to get done a little quicker!"

A Consuming Role

When John Cleese, writer-star of the 1988 comedy *A Fish Called Wanda*, held a casting call for the title role, he didn't know it would spell death for most of the auditioning fish.

"We had several acting fish that we were planning to try out," Cleese recalled. "But one morning, we walked over to the tank and realized that this one particular fish had eaten thirty-two of the extras!

"She must have wanted the part very badly to have disposed of the competition in that way. It was actually more characteristic of an agent than an actor. We gave her the part. We figured that if we didn't, she might try to eat us also."

The Reel Story

Some classic movie scenes aren't all that they seem to be. For instance:

✶ In the 1953 Western *Shane*, Jack Palance won an Oscar nomination for his role as a hired gunslinger. He oozed a chilling demeanor whenever he mounted or dismounted his horse. But Palance was actually nervous around horses and had trouble getting on and off them.

After much practice, the actor finally made a perfect dismount. So director George Stevens used that shot for all the other scenes requiring Palance's dismounting. Stevens even used it for the actor's mounting as well—by running the film in reverse!

For another scene, the script called for Palance to gallop into town. But when the cameras rolled, he could barely hold on to the reins for dear life. So Stevens told Palance to try a slower canter. However, that didn't look much better. Finally, in resignation, the director told him simply to walk the horse into town. Ironically, it became one of the most memorable scenes in the movie.

✶ Sally Kellerman got her first big movie break by portraying Hot Lips Houlihan in the 1970 war comedy *M*A*S*H*. Her famous nude scene—in which actors Donald Sutherland and Elliott Gould pull down the sides of her shower tent as she screams in surprise—was achieved with a little devious trick.

Because Kellerman was shy and expressed reservations about the scene, director Robert Altman was afraid she couldn't pull it off without some assistance. So without her knowledge, Altman arranged for the entire cast to remove their clothing and stand off-camera. When the tent came down, Sally turned to the camera, suddenly saw her fellow cast members as naked as she was—and screamed in genuine surprise. It looked so good, Altman didn't even order a retake.

✶ Although Marilyn Monroe was delightful in the 1959 screwball comedy *Some Like It Hot,* she was difficult to direct, often unsure of her lines, and frequently late on the set. Incredibly, she often needed forty or more takes even for the simplest of scenes.

One scene in which Monroe walks into Tony Curtis's room, says, "Where's the bourbon?" and looks for the bottle in a bureau required more than fifty takes! She either moved off cue, froze on her line, or, in most cases, blew her line. "On the fifty-third take," recalled director

Billy Wilder, "I told her we had put her line on pieces of paper and they were in every drawer she would open. So what happened? She went to the wrong piece of furniture!" Only after the fifty-fourth take did she do the scene right—with the help of a cheat sheet.

Foul Play

Hearing-impaired actress Marlee Matlin, who played a deaf assistant district attorney on TV's "Reasonable Doubts," tutored her co-star Mark Harmon and other cast members in some sign language—how to swear!

"When I first met everybody, I taught them the dirty signs," said Matlin, who lost her own hearing after an illness when she was eighteen months old. "It's a good way to break the ice."

A Winters Blunderland

Shelley Winters was so dumbstruck playing opposite Oscar-winner Ronald Colman in the 1947 movie *A Double Life* that she nearly blew her first big role.

Shelley's first day on the set was a disaster. When director George Cukor introduced her to Colman, the young actress was too awestruck to think or move. She could barely do or say even the simplest of things without screwing up.

They rehearsed their first scene for an hour: Colman sits down in a restaurant and Winters, playing a waitress, pours him a cup of coffee and hands him a menu. Then she pours him a glass of ice water and takes out her pad and pencil while he looks over the menu. "How is the chicken cacciatore?" he asks. She replies, "Well, it's *your* stomach." It was a simple scene.

"We did ninety-six takes—a record for those days," Winters recalled. "Everything that could go wrong went wrong.

"I broke my pencil. I dropped my pad. I stumbled in. I poured coffee on Ronald Colman's hands. I poured coffee on his lap. I couldn't believe what was happening. I poured water in his glass and forgot to stop and it overflowed. Then I broke the glass. In the next take, I dropped the pitcher. It was a nightmare. I had the wardrobe department and four prop men cleaning up after me.

"After countless takes, I realized that I just could not function. Ronald Colman's presence paralyzed me."

Finally, Cukor called for a lunch break. Graciously, Colman asked Winters to have lunch with him. He asked her questions about herself and told her stories about his life.

"I began to loosen up," Winters recalled. "When we got back to the set, he was still Ronald Colman, but he was my friend. We went back to work and I did the scene technically perfect. I will always be grateful to Ronald Colman. He made me relax at lunch and by doing that, he saved my role—and perhaps even my career."

Skirting the Issue

Christina Applegate made the crew's day on the "Married . . . with Children" set.

During a rehearsal in 1990, a scene called for the actress, who plays daughter Kelly on the TV sitcom, to unzip her skirt. But just as she started to pull the zipper down, she heard the director yell, "Drop it!"

So that's exactly what she did—and ended up red-faced, with her skirt around her ankles and the cast and crew in stitches. It turned out that the director was just telling a stagehand to drop a lighting cable.

No Ball For This Belle

No one bungled a major audition the way Lucille Ball did.

In 1939, when producer David O. Selznick was casting for Hollywood's most sought-after female role—Scarlett O'Hara in the epic film *Gone With the Wind*—Lucy was asked to audition. At the time, she was an unknown young actress on the RKO Studios payroll.

The starlet was so excited she bought a new southern-style outfit—a chiffon dress and big hat in a matching flower print. But shortly after she hopped into her yellow convertible, the skies opened up—and it poured buckets. That wouldn't have been a problem, except Lucy couldn't get the top up and she was soaked by the time she arrived at Selznick-International Studios. According to Lucy's memoirs:

"When I got to the studio, the car looked like a swimming pool on wheels. I opened the door to get out, and the flood almost knocked two people over. I made my way up to Selznick's office like a drowned rat. The hat was drooping around my head, the dress was ruined."

Because Selznick was going to be late, his secretary let Lucy sit in his office to dry off in front of a fire. The secretary then gave the drenched actress several shots of brandy to ward off the chill.

"By the time Selznick came in, I was smashed," Lucy recalled. "He asked me to do the scene I had prepared. I was reading Scarlett's speech to Ashley looking like I went over Niagara Falls in a barrel. Selznick was very polite, but even in my stupor I could tell it wasn't going over very well."

After she finished, Selznick told her, "You were very brave to do the scene on your knees like that!"

Only then did the tipsy Lucy realize she had been reading for the part while kneeling the whole time—and never even knew it!

Needless to say, she didn't get the role.

Stick 'em Up!

Edward G. Robinson kept a shamefully sticky secret.

Although Robinson became famous for playing gangsters, he didn't entirely enjoy those roles.

One reason was because he hated the sound of gunfire and would wince whenever he fired a shot. "Every time he squeezed the trigger, he would screw up his eyes," complained director Mervyn Le Roy. "Take after take, he would do the same thing."

So how did Le Roy solve the problem? The makeup man had to tape Robinson's eyelids to make sure that they wouldn't blink when he fired his gun!

. . . But No Coat Hangers

In her prime, Joan Crawford was one of the most demanding actresses ever.

When she arrived at a hotel, the Oscar-winning star— who won the Academy Award for Best Actress for her title role in the 1945 film *Mildred Pierce*—required:

* Toasted French bread, slightly burned on top, waiting in her room.
* Seven packs of cigarettes, four closed, three opened.
* A licensed engineer on duty twenty-four hours a day.
* Management to tell her the exact number of steps from her room to the elevator.

Alan Who?

Here's how actor Alan Arkin describes the fickleness of a Hollywood career: "First," Arkin explained, "it's 'Who's Alan Arkin?' Then it's, 'Get me Alan Arkin!' Next it's, 'He's too expensive. Get me an Alan Arkin type.' Just after that it's, 'Get me a young Alan Arkin.' And then, finally, it's 'Who's Alan Arkin?'"

Sob Story

During the filming of Merle Oberon's deathbed scene for the 1939 movie *Wuthering Heights,* David Niven suffered one of his most mortifying moments ever when he failed to sob.

No matter how hard he tried, he couldn't muster up any tears. Finally, after several ruined takes, frustrated director William Wyler called in the prop man, who proceeded to spray menthol through a handkerchief into Niven's eyes to water them up.

"Bend over the corpse," Wyler instructed Niven. "Now make your crying face . . . blink your eyes . . . heave your shoulders." Niven dutifully did what he was told.

But no tears streamed down the actor's face. What did stream down instead was mentholated slime from his nose.

It was so gross that Oberon, who was supposed to be dead, leaped from her deathbed, shouting, "Oh, how horrid!" and fled to her dressing room, leaving the snotty-nosed Niven totally embarrassed.

Pranks For the Memories

The Madcap Jokesters of Tinseltown

Newman's Own Practical Jokes

At the height of his career, Paul Newman loved pulling practical jokes—especially on his directors. Three of his favorite targets were George Roy Hill, John Huston, and Robert Altman.

Once, Newman was annoyed that he couldn't reach Hill after repeated phone calls. So the actor went to the director's Universal Studios' office—and cut his desk in half with a chain saw! "Hill answered my calls after that," Newman recalled.

A month later, the star received a bill from Universal for a new desk. Newman puckishly responded through his attorney, "It's true I damaged the desk, and I should pay for a new one. But since I am paying for a new one, the old one is mine—and I'm renting it to Hill for $60 a week, which makes Universal in arrears by $300."

During filming of *The Mackintosh Man*, Newman gave Huston a terrible fright. Before doing a scene on a parapet of a tower, Newman arranged with his wardrobe man to stage an argument with him on the tower. They began grappling with each other while the director watched helplessly below. Then, to Huston's shock, Newman appeared to fall off. Just as the panic-stricken director was convinced his star was dead, he discovered that what had plunged off the parapet was just a dummy dressed like Newman. "Huston nearly had a heart attack," the actor recalled with pride.

Newman was on the receiving end of a prank during the filming of *Buffalo Bill and the Indians*. Director Robert Altman had filled Newman's on-location trailer with popcorn from floor to ceiling. So Newman got even when they finished shooting the movie.

One night dozens of friends and acquaintances showed up unexpectedly at Altman's house. They all had received invitations to his party—one that the director knew nothing about. A week later, Altman was inundated with actors who wanted to be cast in his next film—even though he wasn't casting yet. A little investigation by the director revealed that Newman had convinced a local TV station to announce that Altman was looking for 2,500 extras.

Three Cheers For "Cheers" Pranks

When each taping ended, the fun-loving cast of TV's perennial hit "Cheers" often turned into a gang of outrageous practical jokesters.

In 1991, Ted Danson, who plays Sam on the show, pulled down the pants of co-star Woody Harrelson in front of the entire cast. So Woody, who portrays the dim-witted barkeep, retaliated. Later that day, while Danson was showering in his dressing room, Woody opened the shower door and had co-star Kirstie Alley, who plays Rebecca, snap a picture of Danson in nothing but his soap suds.

"It was a good photo," said Harrelson. "I took it around and showed it to everyone who happened by. I showed it to about 150 people just to get even with him."

Danson soon got his revenge on Kirstie. A day after winning her first Emmy as best actress in a TV comedy, Kirstie was upset when the new "Cheers" script revealed that her character was being killed off. She immediately called the producers but was told they were in a meeting and couldn't be disturbed.

So Kirstie raced down to the studio and was confronted by the entire cast and crew, who wore long faces—until they all burst out laughing. Then Danson told their sheepish co-star that the script was a fake. The joke was on her.

Rhea Perlman, who portrays acid-tongued Carla, also has been "pranked" by her co-stars. During a 1992 rehearsal, she opened the door to the bar—and found herself staring at the bare butts of Danson, Harrelson, and George Wendt (Norm on the show). The guys were bent over, warbling "Moon River." Rhea laughed so hard she literally fell down.

French Fried

Glenn Ford pulled a prank that backfired so badly he nearly wound up serving in the French Foreign Legion!

In 1952, while filming *The Green Glove* in Marseilles, France, Ford and several cast members were partying when they decided to join the French Foreign Legion as a joke.

"We all crowded into a taxi and went down to the Foreign Legion headquarters," Ford recalled. "I walked up first, signed my name, and took the oath. But when I turned around, the others had disappeared. They had chickened out.

"The next morning, I found myself in a large barracks with forty other men—all waiting to be issued uniforms and shipped to North Africa. I figured once I explained what happened, they'd let me go. I told an officer, 'Look, I was only kidding. You made a mistake.' And he replied, 'No, my friend. If anybody has made a mistake, you have!'"

Production on the film came to a grinding halt for three days while producers frantically tried to get Ford released from the Legion. They finally convinced the local commandant that keeping Ford in the Legion would put about 120 French movie technicians out of work. So the star's enlistment papers were torn up.

"The very next day I went back to work on *The Green Glove,* a much wiser man and a much wiser actor," said Ford.

Having a Coffin Fit

Actress Melanie Griffith was nearly scared to death from a devilish joke by funnyman Alan King during filming of *The Bonfire of the Vanities.*

The comic, who played Melanie's husband in the movie, died in the film. For the funeral, a lifelike wax figure of King was used as a stand-in to spare him from lying in a casket for hours while the scene was shot.

The cameras were rolling as a sobbing Melanie leaned over to kiss the wax figure in the coffin. Suddenly, she let out a bloodcurdling scream as the "dead man" sprang to life and grabbed her. King had sneaked into the coffin when Melanie wasn't looking to give her the shock of her life!

Sweet Revenge

On the sets of many TV sitcoms, some of the funniest moments occur behind the scenes when stars who are targeted for pranks later seek revenge. For instance:

★ "Wonder Years" star Fred Savage, who plays Kevin, rigged up a bucket filled with sticky cherry soda that would spill on the head of Jason Hervey (his brother on the show) when he opened his dressing-room door. But what Fred didn't know was that Jason had spotted him setting up the gag.

After Fred left, Jason spilled some soda in the doorway to make it appear that he had fallen for the gag. Then he got a stagehand to call Fred into the room. Fred rushed in—and was drenched with the rest of the soda. Laughed Jason: "That'll teach you!"

★ After Candice Bergen took off her shoes at a "Murphy Brown" rehearsal, prankster Joe Regalbuto, who plays Frank, slipped a fake mouse into one of them. When Candice went to put her shoes back on, she screamed with fright as Joe doubled over in laughter.

But Candice got even. The next day, as the cast posed for a publicity shot, she hid Joe's toupee!

✳ Betty White went ape after she walked into her dressing room and found a real live gorilla! She let out a shriek, triggering a roar of laughter from her "Golden Girls" co-stars who had put the tame, trained beast there as a joke on the animal-loving star. "I nearly jumped out of my skin," admitted Betty.

Kissing Fools

Some of Hollywood's best pranks are pulled during the taping of kissing scenes on TV sitcoms. For instance:

✳ During the first year of "Full House," John Stamos couldn't wait to kiss co-star Lori Loughlin. That's because before the scene, Stamos would eat garlic and onions and then watch Lori gag during their smooch. The producers finally told Stamos to hold the onions, hold the garlic.

✳ Before taping a kissing scene in front of a live studio audience in 1990, "Growing Pains" star Kirk Cameron rubbed his lips with a pain reliever for teething babies that produces a hot, numbing sensation. He then planted a long lip lock on co-star Chelsea Noble. The surprised actress let out a wail, clutched her mouth, and hollered, "My lips are on fire!"

Kirk shrugged and told the baffled audience, "I must be hot stuff." Then he fessed up to the prank and tossed Chelsea a wet towel as the audience roared.

Dead Again

The death of actor John Barrymore triggered one of Hollywood's most shameful, funniest—and macabre—pranks of all time.

Barrymore and fellow swashbuckling actor Errol Flynn were the best of friends and drinking buddies. When Barrymore died in 1942, Flynn and his pals held an Irish wake in the funeral home.

After a few too many toasts, Flynn staggered out of the funeral home to meet a friend. Meanwhile, his buddies, led by director Raoul Walsh and actor Peter Lorre, conjured up a sick practical joke.

For a few hundred dollars, they bribed a young funeral attendant to lend them Barrymore's body for a couple of hours and smuggled his corpse from its coffin to Flynn's house. There, they propped the body in a chair in front of the fireplace and put a drink in his hand. Then they hid in the house and waited for Flynn to show up.

When the unsuspecting Flynn came home, he flicked on the lights, threw his hat and coat on the chair, and walked across the room. He nodded at Barrymore, took about three steps, and froze. "Oh my God!" he shouted.

Later, recalling the prank to reporters, Flynn said, "Can you imagine the shock I felt after being at Jack's wake and to come home and find that son of a bitch sitting there in my favorite chair with a drink in his hand?

"I aged thirty years on the spot. It scared the living bejesus out of me. But you know what I did? I just sat down in the chair next to him and had a drink with Jack."

His friends were dying laughing and joined him in a toast to Barrymore. "We all had a big laugh," said Flynn. "It was the crazy sort of thing that Jack would have appreciated."

One Hall of a Prank

Hip late-night talk show host Arsenio Hall has gained a reputation as an easy mark for practical jokesters.

Once, in 1991, he left a Los Angeles nightclub and asked for his car. The attendant pulled up in a beat-up old Chevy. The shocked Arsenio protested that his car wasn't a junker but a sparkling new white Jaguar.

"Well, I did see a woman just a minute ago drive off in a white Jag," said the attendant. "It was the only one in the parking lot."

Convinced that someone had stolen his car, Arsenio fretfully told the attendant to call the police. Just then, his white Jaguar pulled up—and out stepped his friend, funnyman Eddie Murphy, laughing like a loon.

ARSENIO HALL

The Day Bob Hope Was (Toe)Nailed

What began as a simple scene in a movie turned into one of the most mortifying moments ever for Bob Hope when he became the victim of a sneaky practical joke.

In 1962, Hope was in London filming *The Road to Hong Kong* with Bing Crosby. One day, while Hope was preparing to do a scene that Crosby wasn't in, Bing headed for the golf course, telling Hope to catch up with him later in the day when the shooting was finished.

"We started to film a harem scene," Hope recalled. "I was surrounded by gorgeous girls who waited on me hand and foot. In fact, one was pretending to give me a pedicure. Or at least that's what I thought at the time."

When the scene was finished at noon, Hope dashed off to the golf course to join Crosby. "We had a great game, then headed for the locker room to shower," Hope recounted. "As I started to take off my shoes and socks while talking to Bing, I heard snickering.

"It grew louder and I looked up to see a bunch of starchy old English types staring at my feet. I looked down—and blinked in absolute shock. I couldn't believe what I was seeing. My toenails on one foot were painted with bright fire-engine-red nail polish!

"It was only a second before the color of my face matched the color of my toenails. And then I looked at Bing, who was rolling around with laughter.

"I knew what had happened. The harem girl had painted my nails for a gag. But when I tried to explain that to the English types, they looked at me like I was a nut. One old guy rolled his eyes heavenward in disgust and said, 'Hollywood!'"

A Heavy Role

During filming of *The Godfather*, Marlon Brando was to do a scene in which he is carried away on a stretcher after being shot.

But when the cameras started rolling, the actors found they could barely lift the stretcher. They knew Brando was heavy, but not that heavy.

Suddenly, the star began laughing. He confessed that when they weren't looking, he had secretly slipped several heavy weights onto the stretcher.

An Arresting Joke

David Niven got himself and producer Mike Todd in trouble with the police over a joke that went awry.

Before leaving New York for London for the on-location shooting of the 1956 film *Around the World in 80 Days*, Niven was asked by Todd to bring along a few of the producer's personal items.

So at the airport in New York, Niven, as a prank, wired a transatlantic cable to Todd that read: "Have suits, cigars, and radios. Can't for the life of me find your heroin."

When Niven arrived in London, he was shocked to find Todd at the airport—in handcuffs. Both Todd and Niven were taken into custody by Scotland Yard police and interrogated about their suspected drug dealings. It took several hours of earnest talking before Niven finally convinced the police that it was all a joke—one that had backfired.

Role Reversal

Dumb Decisions that Stars Lived to Regret

Coulda, Woulda, Shoulda

Some of the most famous roles on television were turned down by actors who lived to regret it. For example:

★ Bing Crosby was the first choice to play the wily, rumpled police detective Columbo. But Der Bingle nixed the idea and the part went to Peter Falk. Commented Falk years later, "It's interesting how, in a month, your choice can go from a good-looking singer with a pipe to a one-eyed actor with a New York accent."

★ In the TV pilot for "Star Trek," Jeffrey Hunter played Captain James Kirk, commander of the Starship *Enterprise*. When the show was picked up as a series, Hunter bowed out because he felt "Star Trek" was no more than an overblown kiddie show. William Shatner then took over the role—but not before he had declined the lead in "Dr. Kildare," which became a hit series and made a star of Richard Chamberlain.

★ Fred MacMurray, of "My Three Sons" fame, turned down the title role of "Perry Mason." Raymond Burr got the part instead—but only after he had read for the role of Mason's rival, prosecutor Hamilton Burger.

✶ Tammy Grimes, who starred on Broadway as a ghost in *High Spirits*, was chosen for the role of the pretty witch Samantha on TV's "Bewitched." But Tammy infuriated producer William Dozier by rejecting the first script and demanding a rewrite. Dozier then dumped her for Elizabeth Montgomery.

✶ Mickey Rooney as Archie Bunker? It could have been if Rooney had said yes to producer Norman Lear. But the actor said no way to portraying America's No. 1 bigot on "All in the Family" because he believed the show would be too offensive for the general viewing public. So the plum role on the now-classic TV show went to Carroll O'Connor.

✶ Matthew Broderick was first offered the part of teenage corporate bigwig wannabe Alex Keaton on "Family Ties." But he declined. So unknown Canadian actor Michael J. Fox was handed the role. But not without controversy. NBC programming chief Brandon Tartikoff felt Fox was wrong for the part and wanted him dumped, predicting, "That's a face you'll never see on a lunchbox."

✶ Van Johnson was set to play Eliot Ness on "The Untouchables." But just two days before the first rehearsal for the pilot, Johnson's wife, acting as his agent, demanded the producers pay the actor $20,000 instead of the $10,000 that he had agreed to earlier. The producers ripped up his contract and gave the part to Robert Stack.

4-Star Mistake

For his vivid portrayal of a redneck sheriff in the 1967 hit movie *In the Heat of the Night*, Rod Steiger won an Academy Award for Best Actor. Ironically, winning that Oscar played a part in his blowing a chance at copping another one.

"I've always been a pacifist," Steiger said. "So, after *In the Heat of the Night*, all my philosophies were reinforced and I was feeling great. Then I was offered [the title role of] *Patton*, and I grandly announced I would not make a movie that glorified war. I was the biggest schmuck who ever lived. It was the great mistake of my career."

When Steiger turned down the role, the part was offered to George C. Scott, whose unforgettable portrayal of the eccentric, temperamental, brilliant four-star General George Patton earned the actor an Oscar—one of seven that the 1970 film won, including Best Picture.

Said Steiger, "If I'd done *Patton*, who knows? I might have gone on and done *The Godfather*."

One-Eyed Joker

When Peter Falk was trying to break into the movies, Columbia Pictures boss Harry Cohn sent him packing because they didn't see eye to eye.

"I was trying to sell him on how great I was," recalled the veteran actor. "He took one look at me and very discreetly tried to bring up the subject of my glass eye." (Falk lost his right eye to cancer when he was three years old and has worn an artificial one ever since.)

61

"Cohn called it my 'deficiency.' I didn't know what he was talking about, so I said, 'What deficiency?' I thought he might have meant vitamins or something. Cohn replied, 'Your eye. You're a little off-center in your vision. It will show on the screen.'

"Well, I finally agreed to a stupid screen test to see if my 'deficiency' would show up on the screen. Cohn called me back to his office and said, 'Thank you, Mr. Falk. But for the same money, I can get an actor with *two* eyes."

Cos and Effect

In 1984, ABC had first crack at buying a new sitcom starring its creator, Bill Cosby, as the head of an upscale black family.

But the network bigwigs passed—believing the show lacked bite and that viewers wouldn't watch an unrealistic portrayal of blacks as wealthy, well-educated professionals.

It was the biggest programming blunder in TV history.

NBC bought "The Cosby Show"—and went on to make a different kind of TV history. The series was such a smash hit that it remained the No. 1 show for four straight years, was a ratings winner throughout its eight-year run, lifted NBC from its ten-year status as a last-place network to first place, resurrected TV comedy, and became the most profitable series ever broadcast.

At the end of the show's first year, a proud Cosby told members of NBC's annual affiliates convention that ABC programmers nixed his comedy because they wanted shows with "more cars flying and tall white men—with mustaches." He added that ABC passed "because all the marketing people said sitcoms were dead. And then, of course, to bring on a black family at a time when sitcoms were dead and black families were dead . . ." Cosby didn't finish his sentence. He just shook his head as the audience erupted in laughter.

Interestingly, NBC turned down the comedy when it was first proposed as a funny show about a blue-collar worker. But then Cosby's wife, Camille, urged the comedian to change the lead characters to upscale professionals, which he did—Cosby playing Dr. Cliff Huxtable, an obstetrician, and Phylicia Rashad portraying his wife Clair, an attorney. The show was again rejected by ABC, but was finally picked up by NBC.

"The concept of the show was that there's a war going on here between parents and children, and we parents have no intention of losing," said Cosby. "From the onset, I wanted to give the house back to the parents."

The landmark sitcom did just that by bringing joy to tens of millions of viewers every Thursday night.

Be-Raft of Any Business Sense

George Raft played plenty of ruthless gangsters in Warner Brothers movies. But when it came to contracts, he was a wide-eyed innocent.

After one too many battles with studio boss Jack Warner, Raft finally decided he wanted out of his studio contract. That was fine with Warner because he felt that Raft's public appeal was diminishing.

Hoping to avoid a long, protracted battle between lawyers and agents and not wanting to pay the $100,000 left on Raft's contract, Warner asked the star, "What do you say that we settle for $10,000?"

"That's fine with me," declared Raft.

But before the movie mogul had a chance to have his secretary prepare the check, he was given a delightful surprise. Raft—showing his complete lack of business acumen—suddenly whipped out his checkbook and wrote a payment to Warner Brothers for $10,000!

Years later, Warner recalled, "I practically ran to the bank with the check before he changed his mind."

Added Raft in a classic understatement, "I was never very good with money."

Coulda, Woulda, Shoulda Part II

Some famous movie stars have turned down memorable roles that made film history. For instance:

✶ Robert Redford said no to the chance to play the title role of Ben Braddock in the 1967 smash hit *The Graduate*. The part went to then-unknown Dustin Hoffman and made him an instant star.

✶ Kirk Douglas gave the thumbs down to the role of Kid Shelleen in the 1965 comic Western *Cat Ballou* because he didn't think it was good for his image to portray a drunken gunfighter. Lee Marvin didn't have a problem with the role. It won him an Academy Award for Best Actor.

✶ Jane Fonda didn't think much of the role of bank-robbing beauty Bonnie Parker and declined the chance to star in the 1967 hit film *Bonnie and Clyde*. Faye Dunaway played the part to critical acclaim.

✶ Steve McQueen was originally supposed to play Sundance in the 1969 hit *Butch Cassidy and the Sundance Kid*. But McQueen, who was a rising star at the time, backed out when his demand to get equal billing with co-star Paul Newman was denied. Robert Redford took his place.

✶ George Raft turned down three of what became Humphrey Bogart's greatest roles. In 1941, Raft was asked to star in *High Sierra* and *The Maltese Falcon*, but the parts were of no interest to him. Then, in 1942, Raft had the chance to play Rick in one of the all-time great movies, *Casablanca*. Again, he said no, much to the appreciation of Bogie.

Hedy Lamarr declined the role of Ilsa in *Casablanca* because the script wasn't finished when she was offered the part. So Ingrid Bergman took over and, with Bogart, made film history.

Myrna Loy rejected the lead opposite Clark Gable in the 1934 classic *It Happened One Night* because she thought the screwball comedy would flop. So the role went to Claudette Colbert, who won an Oscar for Best Actress—one of five given the movie, including Best Picture.

W.C. Fields could have played the title role in *The Wizard of Oz*, one of America's favorite films. In fact, the part was written for Fields, who would have portrayed the wizard as a cynical con man. But Fields wanted more than the $75,000 MGM offered him, so character actor Frank Morgan filled in.

Wheel of Misfortune
Wacky Mishaps on the Set

V_NN_ WH_T_'S M_ST _MB_RR_SS_NG M_M_NT

During a 1990 "Wheel of Fortune" taping in front of a live audience, the world of Vanna White went topsy turvy.

Vanna was energetically twisting and turning letters in a slinky strapless dress when suddenly . . . RRRIIIPPP! Her zipper broke open all the way down her back. Before she could utter a gasp, the front of her dress fell as the audience stared in wide-eyed astonishment.

Vanna yanked the dress up over her half bra and raced offstage. She returned moments later to an ovation in a new dress.

Singer Linda Ronstadt can sympathize with Vanna. During a concert in 1990, Linda was belting out a song when the petticoat under her dress suddenly fell to the stage. Being the trouper that she was, Linda kicked it aside and continued singing without missing a beat. Afterwards, she confided to friends, "I've never been so embarrassed."

VANNA WHITE

Making a Big Splash

Gregory Peck—one of Hollywood's most respected actors—took on a role that, for one memorable scene, was way over his head.

Portraying famous World War II general Douglas MacArthur in the 1977 film *MacArthur*, Peck was supposed to step out of a landing craft onto the shore of the Philippines and say those immortal words, "I have returned."

The scene—which accurately reflected what really happened when the general arrived—called for the president of the Philippines to be on the craft with the general. On that historic day, the ramp was lowered and MacArthur and the president were set to go ashore.

"I hope that the waters aren't too deep," said the president. "My people will find out that I can't swim."

"I wouldn't worry about that, Mr. President," replied MacArthur. "My people will find out that I can't walk on water."

With the cameras rolling, the actors played the scene to perfection—until it came time for Peck to step out of the landing craft.

"Somebody had forgotten to measure the water's depth at that spot," Peck recalled. "So when I stepped off the ramp, I dropped into water that was more than five feet deep. I lost my balance and sank like a rock beneath the waves.

"I disappeared for a few seconds, and the cameras focused on my hat as it floated to shore. Then I came up spluttering and laughing, and I waded ashore like a wet Labrador.

"It was a ridiculous sight—and my most embarrassing moment."

A 'Buffo' Performance

Julio Iglesias—one of the world's most popular and romantic singers—was literally caught with his pants down after a boffo performance.

It happened in Stockholm, Sweden, on the last leg of his worldwide concert tour in 1984. Iglesias had arrived back at his posh hotel suite, bleary-eyed, tired, and looking forward to a long, sound sleep. He stripped down to his shorts and was ready to hop into bed when he realized that he had forgotten to leave a card with his breakfast order outside the door.

So he filled out the card and, still clad in just his briefs, walked out into the deserted hall. Suddenly, he heard a "click," and discovered that the door had locked behind him.

"I knocked on the door of the room beside me," the singer recalled. "A white-haired man of about seventy opened it, took one look at me standing there almost naked, and started hurling insults at me. Then he slammed the door."

Iglesias knew it was futile to go knocking on doors. So he figured the only sensible thing to do was head for the front desk and get a new key—and pray that no one would see him.

"I walked to the elevator and pushed the 'lobby' button—but then wished I hadn't," Iglesias recalled. "I began to worry. My panic grew as each floor flashed by. I feared the dozens of photographers who'd been in the lobby earlier would still be there. My knees felt like jelly and my heart was in my throat."

When the elevator doors opened, Iglesias peeked out and was relieved to see that the lobby was empty except for the night clerk. Taking a deep breath, the singer scurried to the front desk and said, "Give me a spare key—and hurry, please."

But before the startled clerk could find a key, the hotel's double doors swung open. "In poured a dozen of the best-dressed theatergoers one could ever meet," Iglesias recalled. "The women were wearing gowns and pearls and the men had on tuxedos and white gloves. They spotted me and stopped dead with their mouths dropped open.

"I squirmed. There was absolutely nothing I could do. They all recognized me at once and one of the women screamed, 'Julio Iglesias! Julio Iglesias!'"

The flustered, red-faced singer grabbed the key from the clerk's outstretched hand and beat a fast retreat into the elevator and back up to his room.

"I didn't sleep a wink," Iglesias said later. "I was tossing and turning with embarrassment over what those people must have thought."

A Car-azy Caper

One day in 1990, actress Michelle Pfeiffer was in the studio parking lot unable to open a car door with her key. So, in frustration, she began beating on the window with her shoe.

But she stopped when a studio executive walked up and demanded to know why she was hitting *his* car. The embarrassed

actress suddenly realized that she had confused his car with hers, which was the same make, model, and color.

After stammering apologies, Michelle autographed her shoe and gave it to the bigwig—and then stumbled off to find *her* car.

The Price is Wrong

Some of the wackiest moments on the popular TV game show "The Price Is Right" were surprise accidents.

"The wildest things imaginable happen in our show," said host Bob Barker. "Because we tape it in its entirety in an hour, we almost always air it just like it is."

One time, a model was sitting at the wheel of a car being offered as a prize. As crew members pushed it from behind, the car smashed through a wall on the set. The camera caught the bedlam—as well as Barker ducking for cover when the wall tumbled down. "But the model never lost her stage presence," Barker recalled. "The car kept rolling and she continued smiling and waving."

Another time, a contestant was supposed to turn a big wooden key to collect his prizes, but the key got stuck. Barker, a karate expert, gave the key a hard kick—and broke it. The audience roared with laughter.

Only once was Barker injured during a show. It happened when a 250-pound woman went berserk after winning a prize.

"In her excitement, she chased me across the stage, picked me up in a bear hug and squeezed me so hard that she injured my ribs," Barker said. "Now when contestants try to corner me or give me a big hug, I try to dodge them."

A Hit Movie

While making the 1946 movie *Gilda*—an emotional drama about a love triangle—stars Glenn Ford and Rita Hayworth had to film a big fight scene.

Before the cameras rolled, director Charles Vidor took Ford aside and, in a whisper, told him not to fake it when he slapped his co-star. So Ford smacked Hayworth hard enough to send the stunned actress reeling.

Later, for another fight scene between the two, Vidor told Hayworth to throw real punches. So she socked Ford four times in the mouth—and knocked out two of his teeth!

Ironically, their physical violence led to physical attraction. During shooting of the film, the two stars fell in love with each other and had a widely publicized affair.

Cruise-ing For Trouble

Tom Cruise nearly crashed in his chips while filming the 1990 racing movie *Days of Thunder.*

During a race scene, Cruise, who did his own stunt driving, had his lines taped to the dashboard. He took his eyes off the road for a split second to look at his cheat sheet when he lost control of the car. Cruise skidded into a concrete wall, smashing up the car. Fortunately, the star wasn't hurt—just embarrassed.

Knock Out Actors

Some actors have been known to knock themselves out in front of the camera—literally.

During filming of *Equinox*, in 1991, star Matthew Modine was doing a scene in which his character grabs a friend, played by actor Paul Meshigian. But in a freak accident, the two actors tripped over each other's feet, fell, and hit their heads on the floor so hard that they were both knocked out cold. They were rushed to the hospital while still unconscious, but they recovered quickly with no ill effects.

If anything, the mishap inspired Modine's sense of humor. Before he returned to the set, he had the makeup department make his face appear swollen and bruised. When the actor went on the set, director Alan Parker took one horrified look at his star and nearly fainted. Modine burst out laughing and said, "Just kidding!"

In 1992, Paul Michael Valley, who portrays Ryan on the TV soap "Another World," was knocked out of this world while taping what should have been a simple scene.

Valley was supposed to slump back onto a sofa. But he was off his mark by about a foot. So instead of going straight back onto the couch, he missed the couch and toppled backwards. Valley banged his head on a fireplace mantle with such force that he was knocked out cold for several minutes.

When he recovered, the actor was woozy and bleeding, so he was whisked to a hospital emergency room. The accident was embarrassing, but what happened next was outrageous.

A fan recognized Valley, who was still on a stretcher—and demanded his autograph! "I'm lying there with blood on my head," Valley recalled, "and this woman comes up to me and says, 'I know this is a bad time . . .' Then she hands me a pen!" Being a nice guy, Valley signed it.

Shutter Bugged

Sylvester Stallone takes pride in doing most of his own stunts, but there was one time when he was too good.

During filming of the 1988 action adventure film *Rambo III*, Sly was supposed to shoot a crossbow arrow directly toward the camera, which was hidden behind a plywood cage. With the lens peeking out from a tiny hole cut in the wood, Stallone aimed for a masking tape "X" that was about a foot above the camera.

Although they knew Stallone was a good shot, no one in the crew expected him to hit the "X." He didn't. From 75 yards away, Sly let it fly, and the arrow landed dead center—right on the $20,000 lens!

The Day Ronald Reagan Was Almost Strangled—By a Chimp!

Ronald Reagan was nearly choked to death by the chimp that appeared with him in the 1951 movie *Bedtime for Bonzo*.

In the film, Reagan plays a professor who treats a chimp, Bonzo, as his child for an experiment. Although man and animal looked cute together on the screen, the cameras didn't reveal that, for some strange reason, the chimp hated Reagan.

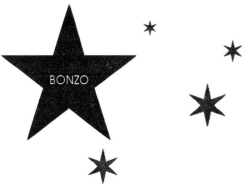

One day, the actor, trying to be friendly with Bonzo, leaned forward to say something soothing to the chimp when the animal grabbed hold of Reagan's tie. Bonzo pulled so hard that the tie tightened around the actor's neck until he couldn't breathe or call for help.

Fortunately, Bonzo's trainer was nearby, saw what was happening, and cut the tie with a pair of scissors just in time. From then on, Reagan never went near the chimp until he had to shoot his scenes with him.

Hollywood Sharks

Jaws—one of the biggest moneymakers in cinema history—was also one of the biggest headaches to film.

That's because the mechanical sharks behaved much like the boat-chomping, man-killing Great Whites they portrayed.

In 1975, director Steven Spielberg shot some of the movie off the coast of Martha's Vineyard with three studio-crafted sharks. The main shark—a twenty-five-foot-long, one-ton monster nicknamed Bruce—was connected to a submerged sea sled operated by scuba divers.

One scene called for the Great White to smash into the fishing boat *Orca*. But the big mechanical shark overacted just a bit. It rammed into the boat with such force that it cracked the hull and sank the vessel!

The cameras and exposed film on board the boat sank thirty feet to the bottom. Remarkably, the cameras and film were saved after they were retrieved and flushed with fresh water. The unexpected sinking scene, filmed from another boat, remained in the finished movie.

During the shooting of *Jaws*, Spielberg became friendly with Walter Cronkite, who was the CBS news anchorman at the time. Cronkite frequently vacationed at Martha's Vineyard.

One day, Spielberg invited Cronkite to watch him film a scene with one of the mechanical sharks. The director proudly explained how the shark was tethered from a long control platform on the ocean floor with hydraulic pistons and compressed air hoses.

The scene called for the shark to leap out of the water. When Spielberg called "Action!," the shark became twisted in a cable and only the tail broke through the surface. Seeing Spielberg's frustration and embarrassment, Cronkite asked the director, "Have you ever considered a career in broadcasting?"

Dick Clark's Record Riot

Dick Clark—one of television's most popular, enduring, and beloved personalities—has hosted so many shows over the years that he's learned to expect the unexpected, often to hilarious results.

Some of the zaniest moments have happened on the TV's longest-running variety show, "American Bandstand."

In 1979, Clark was about to introduce the singing duo Ashford and Simpson when he received word that Valerie Simpson was missing. A member of the crew finally found her—trapped in the ladies' room! She couldn't get the door open because it was stuck. Simpson had been screaming and pounding on the door for twenty minutes before she was discovered. With just sixty seconds before airtime, a stagehand grabbed a fire axe and chopped the door down. Simpson, the pro that she was, regained her composure and made it in front of the cameras just in the nick of time.

GEORGE
BURNS

The venerable George Burns lived up to his last name—literally—when he appeared on the show. He walked out to a standing ovation, not knowing that one of his famous cigars—which he thought he had put out in his dressing room—had just ignited a fire in a wastebasket. So while Burns began to sing a little ditty, a quick-thinking stagehand grabbed a fire extinguisher and doused the blaze.

In the show, stars lip-synched their hits, often to unintentionally hilarious results. One time, country singer Jimmy Dean was in front of the audience and got the surprise of his life because the wrong record was being played. Instead of Jimmy Dean's song, a record by male black artist Dee Clark was spun.

Another time, Paul Anka was lip-synching his hit "Diana" when the needle got stuck in the grooves of the record as he was holding a long note. Dick Clark later told a reporter, "Paul cracked up with laughter as his recorded voice seemed to hold that note forever—and that was something I'll never forget."

Technical (Under)Achievement Awards

Ridiculous Movie Gimmicks

Scaring Up Customers

No producer came up with more zany "technical achievements" in filmdom than William Castle.

He introduced his first inane innovation—Emergo—in the 1958 movie *The House on Haunted Hill*. Vincent Price played a mad zillionaire who offered people $50,000 each if they could make it through the night in a spooky old mansion.

At a critical point in the film, Price turned a handle. Suddenly, in the theater, a skeleton leapt from near the screen, soared over the stunned audience and disappeared into the balcony in the back. That was Emergo.

The skeleton was inflatable and made of illuminated plastic that slid along two trolley wires from the screen to the balcony. The original concept needed refinement. During a screening with studio executives, a fifteen-pound skeleton slipped off its wires and crashed into one of the bigwigs.

For the film's national distribution, 1,000 inflatable skeletons were made and the motors and wires were installed in theaters willing to try Emergo.

Was it a hit? That depends on your definition of hit. According to a contemporary account in the *Saturday Evening Post*, "Breakage has been high, for as the balloonlike skeletons wing overhead, they present irresistibly attractive targets to small boys with slingshots."

The following year, Castle conjured up another nutty technical advance—Percepto. It was a real shocker. Moviegoers in selected seats actually received an electrical shock!

In the 1959 film *The Tingler*, Vincent Price discovers that fear causes a creepy-crawly creature to grow on people's spines. This nasty organism shatters the vertebrae of its victims unless they scream for their lives.

Here's how Percepto worked: In a scene toward the end of the film, the monster sneaks into a movie theater. But then, in real life, the screen goes blank. Now in total darkness, the audience hears Price's voice on the sound track announce: "Ladies and gentlemen, please do not panic! But scream! Scream for your lives! The Tingler is loose in *this* theater, and if you don't scream, it may kill you!"

Meanwhile, paid girls planted in the audience begin screaming and fainting while on the sound track voices shriek, "It's on me!" "Help!" and "Look out, it's under your seat!" That's when Percepto kicks in. Low-voltage motors hooked up to the bottom of the theater seats shock the patrons. The real shock to moviegoers was that they had paid their money to see such a dreadful film.

In 1961, Castle came up with another goofy gimmick—the Punishment Poll.

Patrons were told they would get to choose the ending of his horror film *Mr. Sardonicus*, which was about a homicidal recluse whose face is frozen in a hideous grin. At the climax of the film, the projector in the theater was turned off and an usher asked the audience to vote on the fate of the mad Mr. Sardonicus. By holding fluorescent "thumb cards" either up or down, the patrons could make "the ultimate choice" of watching an ending in which the madman lives or one in which he dies. Naturally, the audience always yelled for death and then watched Sardonicus perish.

It was a good thing they chose death. Castle was so confident of their choice that he only filmed the one ending.

A Horror-ible Idea

Producer-director Hy Averback came up with a daffy device to lure scaredy-cats into theaters to see his bloody 1966 flick *Chamber of Horrors*.

Knowing that many people hate scary surprises, Averback created an innovation just for them—the Horror Horn and the Fear Flasher.

Because the movie was about a mad killer on the loose at a wax museum, it featured plenty of blood and guts. However, at key moments in the film, a loud horn on the sound track would blare and a red warning light on the film would flash to alert squeamish patrons to close their eyes. That way, they could avoid watching particularly gory scenes that followed.

But the Horror Horn and the Fear Flasher didn't bolster the box office take, mainly because the movie was considered so awful. More often than not, the Horror Horn did nothing more than awaken bored patrons who were dozing off during the lame film.

A Reel Stink Bomb

There was one big problem with the technical achievement known as Smell-O-Vision.

It stunk.

Michael Todd Jr., developing the gimmick created by his late father, produced the first feature film in which actual smells were released into the theater to coincide with scenes on the screen. His 1960 movie *The Scent of Mystery* featured more than fifty different aromas, from roses to wood shavings, gun smoke to peppermint.

Smell-O-Vision was pumped from a main system that kept the different essences under pressure in metal vials. The scents were released through plastic tubes attached to each seat and were neutralized four seconds later by the release of an odorless chemical.

The two most important aromas critical to the movie were those of perfume from a mystery woman and the pipe tobacco of the bad guy. One of the problems with Smell-O-Vision was that it often wasn't synchronized with the action on the screen. As an embarrassing result, when one of the actors was talking about smelling the perfume, the audience was sniffing garlic.

The critics stuck their noses in the air. Said *Time* magazine, "Most customers will probably agree that the smell they liked the best was the one they got during intermission—fresh air."

The Scent of Mystery with Smell-O-Vision played only in Chicago, New York, and Los Angeles, and would have been a big money-loser if Todd hadn't rereleased it under the new title *Holiday in Spain*—without the smells.

Todd's stinky film wasn't the only smellie around. A 1959 documentary of China, *Behind the Great Wall*, featured Aroma-Rama in which smells were released through the theater's air conditioning system. But there was a problem. The blowers that wafted all the scents into the theater failed to suck them back in. Soon, the theater was full of a sickening mixture of smells that had audiences gagging.

Hallucinogenic Hypnovision

It was called Hallucinogenic Hypnovision. But it was closer to hallucinating hype.

The innovation was conjured up by producer-director-actor Dennis Steckler in the 1963 low-budget horror film *The Incredibly Strange Creatures Who Stopped Living and Became Mixed-Up Zombies* (later retitled *The Teenage Psycho Meets Bloody Mary*). It's about the hideous goings-on at a carny sideshow. As one critic so nicely put it, "This truly bizarre film features awful acting, hideous dialogue, and little plot."

It also featured Hallucinogenic Hypnovision, touted in newspaper ads this way: "Warning! Unlike Anything Before! You Are Surrounded by Monsters! Not 3-D, But Real FLESH AND BLOOD MONSTERS ALIVE! NOT FOR SISSIES! DON'T COME IF YOU'RE CHICKEN!"

So what was this bloodcurdling technical achievement? At certain intervals throughout the movie, a spiraling "hypnotic wheel" suddenly appeared on the screen. This was the cue for theater ushers to run up and down the aisles wearing bloody, glowing masks while waving cardboard axes at people in the audience.

The few screams that came from the audience weren't from fright, but from laughter at the silliness of it all.

All Hyped Up
Outrageous Film Promotions

Plastered Cast

It was supposed to be a cute promotion for Walt Disney's new animated feature, *Pinocchio*. But it looked more like *The Munchkins Meet Animal House*.

At the 1940 premiere in New York, the Disney publicity department decided to hype the movie by hiring a cast of eleven midgets. They were dressed in Pinocchio outfits—complete with long noses—and told to frolic about on top of a theater marquee on Broadway. The midgets danced and sang to the delight of the crowd below, especially the children.

At lunchtime, food and drinks were passed up to the midgets. Unknown to the publicity officials, a friend of the little people secretly sent up to them several quarts of whiskey and gin.

By midafternoon, the Pinocchios were smashed out of their minds. They began belching and making nasty wisecracks to the stunned parents and children below. But the real shock came when some of the midgets put on a strip show from atop the marquee while others rolled dice.

By now, the Times Square crowd had grown so large it spilled out into the street, stopping traffic. Disney officials had been hoping for attention—but not like this. When the drunken midgets refused to come down, the police brought ladders and physically removed the tipsy Pinocchios one by one.

Laughing All the Way to the (Sperm) Bank

For bad taste, it's hard to beat the promotional contest staged to hype the 1992 film *Frozen Assets*, a comedy about a sperm bank.

In the movie, Corbin Bernsen, of "L.A. Law" fame, plays a profit-driven executive who accepts a job sight unseen as a bank president, only to discover that it's a *sperm* bank. Shelley Long plays a humanitarian biologist at the bank. They clash when he tries to increase deposits by running a "Stud of the Year" contest in which the man with the highest sperm count wins $100,000.

The fertile minds of the marketing people behind this universally panned movie decided to hold an identical "Stud of the Year" contest in real life, offering a free Caribbean cruise to the winner. After forty-five entrants submitted samples to producers, the contest reached a climax when Francisco Ferreira, twenty-five, of New York, won with a sperm count of 275 million per millimeter.

Said *Entertainment Weekly* magazine, in announcing the winner, "We're not sure we want to shake his hand."

God Will Get You For That

In 1991, Miramax Pictures distributed the movie *The Pope Must Die*, but newspapers and the three major television networks refused to use the title in ads, fearing it was too offensive.

In the R-rated movie—a spoof on the Vatican—a bumbling priest, played by rotund British comic Robbie Coltrane, accidentally is elected Pope and is targeted for death by underworld agents who want to take over the Vatican.

But moviegoers of all faiths stayed away in droves. So, in desperation, Miramax publicists tried to capitalize on the controversy over the film's title. The company stooped to changing the title to *The Pope Must Diet*, hoping fans would find it more to their taste.

"Someone went around to theaters with chalk and added the 'T' to the end of the title over my picture," said the chubby actor. "I can't take the credit for the name change. I can only take credit for my ample weight."

Did the alternate title work? Fat chance.

Creating a Fuhrer

To promote the 1962 movie *Hitler*, distributors sank to a new low in sensitivity—by helping theater owners sponsor a Fuhrer look-alike contest!

Each lucky winner would win free passes to the film, along with the chance to hold a part-time job to hype *Hitler* at the theater. The best part of the job, promoters told wanna-be dictators, was that you got to wear a Nazi uniform, German Army medals, and, if you didn't already sport one, a false Hitlerian mustache.

The promotion showed such a shocking lack of compassion for the feelings of Holocaust survivors and their families, that a trade magazine sarcastically suggested that the fake Hitlers spread the word about the film by goose-stepping in crowded areas close to the theater or by riding in a convertible, giving the stiff-armed Nazi salute, and shouting "Heil Hitler!"

For rational-thinking moviegoers, the promotion was strictly thumbs down.

Let's See You Worm Out of This One

For the 1977 horror flick *The Worm Eaters*, what better way to plug the movie than by holding worm-eating demonstrations in front of gagging crowds?

That's exactly what the producer and director did.

In the film, a wacko worm breeder turns the townspeople into hideous "worm people" by slipping a few nasty creepy crawlers into their food. In gross close-ups, the audience gets to watch the actors chomp away on live worms.

To attract attention for the film, producer Ted Mikels and director-star Herb Robins went on the road, hoping to disgust fans into watching the movie. At malls, shopping centers, and in front of theaters, Robins and Mikels stood in front of TV cameras and hundreds of grossed-out onlookers and gobbled down live, wriggly eight-inch-long Canadian night crawlers.

Mikels and Robins declared their disgusting stunt so successful that they staged a worm-eating contest in Las Vegas and offered free admission to anyone who ate a worm before entering the theater.

For most patrons, the promotion was just too hard to swallow.

No Weigh to Treat a Lady

Believing that people are willing to hold themselves up to ridicule for a free ticket, producer Frances Millard announced that all women weighing 200 pounds or more would be admitted without charge to his movie *Criminally Insane.*

The 1974 bloodfeast featured a cannibalistic killer—"250 pounds of psychopathic fury!" headlined the movie posters—known as Fat Ethel, who dismembers her victims with a meat cleaver.

At many theaters, scales were set up in front of the box office for hefty women who were willing to trade their dignity for a free ticket. Such a woman had to stand on the scale to prove to management—and the line of cheering, waiting patrons— that she indeed was a 200-pound-plus porker.

Some theater owners tried to be a little more discreet. They simply eyeballed large women and guessed at which ones looked like they weighed enough. It's not known what happened to those owners who mistakenly offered free tickets to indignant overweight women who weren't heavy enough to qualify for the demeaning promotion.

Freebie Jeebies

In an effort to hype their blood-and-gore movies, producers have offered filmgoers everything from free "Up-Chuck Cups" to free burial insurance. For example:

✴ As patrons entered the theater for the 1972 psycho-on-the-loose slasher film *I Dismember Mama*, they were given little paper cups that said, "UP-CHUCK CUP: KEEP IT HANDY. It may be required on short notice during the showing of *I Dismember Mama*."

✴ The 1972 film *The Night of a Thousand Cats* featured a mad millionaire who turned his band of finicky felines into killer kitties by training them to devour the flesh off screaming humans. To make this movie seem much more frightening than it really was, the distributors ran ads promising "BURIAL INSURANCE! If you die from fright or nausea during the performance, we will give you a nice but simple funeral free of charge."

✴ In 1968, producers of the triple feature *Curse of the Living Dead, Revenge of the Living Dead,* and *Fangs of the Living Dead* offered free psychiatric care for disturbed patrons of these horror flicks.

✴ Huge newspaper ads showed a photo of a Charles Manson clone with the caption: "WARNING: This is John Austin Frazier. It has been reported that he now resides at a mental hospital, the result of attending our triple horror program. Because of this tragic event, we, the producers, have secured an insurance policy insuring the sanity of each and every patron. If you lose your mind as a result of viewing this explosion of terror, you will receive *free* psychiatric care or be placed *at our expense* in an asylum for the rest of your life!"

The Hollywood Walk of Shame

✳ Patrons were offered a chance to win "a live rat for your mother-in-law" before a showing of the 1972 verminfest *The Rats Are Coming! The Werewolves Are Here!*—a story about a family of werewolves who raise man-eating rats as a hobby.

After writer-director Andy Milligan used hundreds of rodents in rat attack scenes, he came up with an outrageous promotion to get rid of them. At major showings of the movie, theater owners held drawings and the "lucky" winners each got to take home a live rodent.

A Bird-Brained Stunt

Paramount publicist Joel Stein thought he had come up with a delightful publicity stunt to promote the new Mae West movie *It Ain't No Sin*, which was about to be released in 1933.

He bought about forty parrots and put them in a room with a record player that kept repeating over and over the name of the film. After a few days, Stein proudly told the studio that he had a squadron of parrots who would say *It Ain't No Sin* on cue.

The execs said that was nice—and then informed him that at the last minute they had retitled the movie to *I'm No Angel.*

Shirley You Jest

Twentieth Century-Fox publicists faked Shirley Temple's birth certificate because they wanted millions of fans to think the child star was younger than she really was.

In the 1930s, Shirley was America's No. 1 box office celebrity for four straight years.

Shirley was five years old in 1934 when she made a brief appearance in her first major film, *Stand Up and Cheer*.

"But instead of telling everyone my real age, the studio publicists told the press and public that I was only four years old," Shirley Temple Black told reporters years later. "They even had a new birth certificate published and they had a doctor sign it.

"Of course, I had no idea what was going on. I didn't know that I was five when I was being told I was four. On my thirteenth birthday, my mother told me I wasn't really twelve that day. She said I was entering my teens. This was a tremendous shock to me because I thought I'd lost a year of my life somehow."

Shirley, who years later became the U.S. Ambassador to the African nation of Ghana, said that the publicists also lied to the public about her fan mail and birthday presents. "The amount of letters I received—about two thousand a week—and the birthday gifts that fans sent—about a thousand each year—were always exaggerated and blown out of proportion. What's funny is that my fan mail and gifts were considerable and there was no need to inflate those numbers."

Boob Job

In 1943, Howard Hughes directed the first sexy Western, *The Outlaw*, which brought a storm of protest from shocked, uptight citizens. The focus of their ire was over the camera time devoted to the ample breasts of Jane Russell, who was making her much-ballyhooed screen debut.

Hughes was locked in censorship battles throughout the country, including Maryland which, at the time, prohibited the film from being shown. In upholding the ban, a Maryland judge claimed Russell's breasts "hung over the picture like a summer thunderstorm spread out over a landscape."

It was a made-to-order quote in the imaginative mind of publicity genius Russell Birdwell. As if to prove the judge's point, when the movie premiered in Hollywood, Birdwell hired skywriters to decorate the southern California skies with a pair of enormous circles with dots in their centers!

Oscar (Fright) Night

Nutty Performances at the Academy Awards

Frankly, Frank, It Was Another Frank

No director was more embarrassed at the Academy Awards than Frank Capra, when he mistakenly tried to accept an Oscar that he didn't win.

In 1933, he directed *Lady for a Day*, a tearjerking drama about a poor apple vendor who is transformed by a softhearted racketeer into an elegant lady. The film became a hit and was nominated for Best Picture, Best Screenwriting, Best Director, and Best Actress. Capra, who had yet to win an award, was ecstatic.

"I kept telling myself that I would win four awards," Capra later said. "No other picture had ever won four awards. I would set a record. Hot damn! I wrote and threw away dozens of acceptance speeches. I ordered my first tuxedo." He even rented a plush home in Beverly Hills just so he would be seen by the Oscar voters.

With his speech carefully tucked into his expensive tux, Capra arrived at the awards banquet brimming with confidence. But ten minutes into the ceremonies, he was slightly taken aback when the Oscar for writing went to *Little Women*. "Guess I'll have to settle for three," the disappointed Capra told his friends at the table.

Then came the award for Best Director. Presenter Will Rogers announced the nominees as Capra's blood raced with anticipation. ". . . And the Best Director of the year is . . ." Rogers opened the sealed envelope and laughed. "Well, well, well, what do you know? I've watched this young man for a long time . . . Saw him come up from the bottom, and I mean the bottom."

Meanwhile, Capra's heart was pounding with joy. It had to be him. At last, his dream of winning an Oscar was about to be realized!

In his famous drawl, Rogers announced, "It couldn't happen to a nicer guy. Come up and get it, Frank!"

Capra's table erupted in cheers as the jubilant director began wedging through the crowded tables toward the podium. As the spotlight searched through the darkened room for the winner, Capra waved his arms and shouted, "Over here!"

But then, suddenly, the spotlight moved away from Capra and beamed down on someone else on the other side of the room—the best director of 1933, Frank Lloyd. As Lloyd, who won for his direction of *Cavalcade*, went up to the dais to receive his Oscar and a hug from Rogers, Capra stood in utter disbelief until someone shouted, "Down in front!"

Recalled Capra, "I began the longest, saddest, most shattering walk of my life. I wanted to crawl under the rug. All my friends at the table were crying."

To make matters worse, his movie didn't win a single award that night. "I decided that if they ever did give me an Oscar, I wouldn't be there to accept," said Capra. "Not me, never again."

But he didn't keep his word. A year later, Capra was back at the Academy Awards. This time, he fulfilled his dream when his film, *It Happened One Night*, won for Best Actor, Best Actress, Best Picture—and Best Director.

And the Winner Is . . . In Jail!

Winning the Oscar usually leads to higher pay and better roles. But for one recipient, it led to the slammer.

The 1982 Academy Awards turned into a bittersweet evening for Polish filmmaker Zbigniew Rybcyznski, whose labor of love, *Tango*, was nominated for Best Animated Short Subject. What should have been one of the greatest nights of his life looked more like a bad Fellini movie.

First, no one could pronounce his name right. Presenter Kristy McNichol butchered his moniker when she read the list of nominees. Then, after opening the envelope, she mangled his name again with, "The winner is Zbigniewski Sky . . . something," and laughed.

Rybcyznski happily bounded up the stage and, through his female interpreter, said, "I made a short film, so I will speak very short . . . I am dreaming that someday I will speak longer from this place." But he never got to finish his acceptance speech.

The director and interpreter kissed, and the orchestra, thinking the winner's speech was over, began playing. But the interpreter raised her hand and announced, "It's not over yet. He has an important message." Meanwhile, co-presenter Matt Dillon tried to push Rybcyznski away. The confused director shook his hand and then kissed McNichol. "It's a Slavic custom," the interpreter told the audience. "We are a very warm people." Then she tried to deliver the message praising Polish leader Lech Walesa and the Solidarity movement.

Once Rybcyznski was ushered off the stage, he was led to the interview room where he told reporters, "I chose to name my film *Tango* because everyday life has its rhythms, but basically life is grotesque."

He quickly found out how grotesque after he stepped outside alone to smoke a cigarette. When he tried to return, a guard refused to allow him back inside. Speaking in what little English he knew, Rybcyznski said, "I have Oscar."

But the guard, who had been warned to be on the lookout for gate-crashers, didn't believe the foreigner who was dressed in a tuxedo and tennis shoes. In frustration, the fed-up director kicked the guard, triggering a scuffle that brought security men to the scene.

Moments later, Rybcyznski found himself hustled off to the hoosegow. There, the Oscar winner asked for the only Hollywood lawyer he had heard of, Marvin Mitchelson. When word reached the famous divorce attorney, he told his secretary, "First, bring me an interpreter and then tell me how to pronounce his name."

The charges were dropped the next day. When reporters asked the director for his reaction to his ordeal, he replied philosophically, "Success and defeat are quite intertwined."

Showing Off His Shortcomings

The 1974 Oscarcast was the most em-bare-assing ever aired. Overshadowing all the winners was a nude man who streaked across the stage in front of a stunned audience and millions of shocked TV viewers.

The man who caused eyes to pop was Robert Opel, an unemployed actor who often streaked for pay at Hollywood parties. Before the show, he had surreptitiously obtained a backstage pass and, dressed in formal attire, blended in with the stars and Academy officials.

Midway in the telecast, Opel ducked unnoticed behind a backstage set and stripped naked. Meanwhile, on stage, David Niven began to introduce Elizabeth Taylor as "a very important contributor to world entertainment and someone quite likely . . ."

Niven's speech was interrupted by screams and laughter as Opel jogged across the stage without a stitch on and flashed a peace sign. Niven was momentarily taken aback by the streaker, but conductor Henry Mancini quickly struck up his orchestra with the strains of "Sunnyside Up." Fast-thinking TV director Marty Pasetta switched to another camera so viewers at home were spared the sight of the streaker's manhood.

By the time Opel had raced offstage, the unflappable Niven turned to the audience and in his suave voice said, "Ladies and gentlemen, that was bound to happen. Just think, the only laugh that man will probably ever get is for stripping and showing off his shortcomings." The theater erupted in laughter and applause.

Meanwhile, security guards scurried backstage and nabbed Opel as he was getting dressed. But rather than haul him off to jail, Academy officials—recognizing the publicity value of his stunt—took Opel, once he was fully clothed, to the pressroom and let him speak to reporters. Then he was released.

Recalled Pasetta, the show's director, "I looked up [at the monitors of his six onstage cameras] and saw the streaker times six. And I can tell you a couple of things about him: The shortcomings mentioned by David Niven were anything but. And he wasn't Jewish."

A gate-crasher managed to enjoy some fame and airtime at the 1961 Oscars.

Stan Berman, who had already gained notoriety by invading parties for astronaut John Glenn and President John F. Kennedy, brazenly made it on stage during the Academy Awards.

After Shelley Winters had just presented an award, Berman suddenly appeared at the podium and announced, "Ladies and gentlemen, I'm the world's greatest gate-crasher and I just came here to present [master of ceremonies] Bob Hope with his 1938 trophy."

Berman then gave Winters, who was laughing through his whole spiel, a little trophy and said, "This is for Bob." Winters accepted it and replied, "I'll give it to him."

When Hope returned to the podium a few minutes later, he quipped, "Who needs Price Waterhouse? All we need is a doorman!"

Presenters Say the Darndest Things

Before presenting the Oscar for Best Song in 1982, Bette Midler, in her first Academy Awards appearance, nearly gave producers a heart attack when she ignored the cue cards and went off on her own zany monologue.

"So this is what it actually feels to be up here," she told the audience. "This is fantastic." Referring to losing out as Best Actress in 1980 for *The Rose*, Bette said, "I've been waiting two years for the Academy to call me up and tell me they made a mistake. But do I bear a grudge? No, no. My heart is as big as the sky and I have a mind that retains nothing. This is the Oscars. We have to be dignified as humanly possible. That is why I have decided to rise to the occasion."

With that said, Bette promptly lifted her breasts with her hands, sending the audience into howls of laughter.

In 1962, after announcing that *The Longest Day* had won for Best Special Effects, the non-nominated Shelley Winters didn't want to hand over the statuette. "This is very hard for an actress to let go of," she explained.

At the 1973 Oscars, Elliott Gould and Isabelle Adjani were presenting the award for Best Film Editing. After reading the names of the nominees, Adjani said, "And the winner is . . ." Just then, Gould piped in, "Indiana, 86 to 68"—the score of the NCAA basketball final.

In 1969, buxom presenter Raquel Welch said, "I'm here for Special Visual Effects." The crowd snickered. Referring to the nominees, she added, "There are two of them." The audience could contain itself no longer and broke up in raucous laughter.

As a presenter at the 1976 Academy Awards, bug-eyed comedian Marty Feldman examined an Oscar statuette and ad-libbed, "It's not Jewish. You can tell." Then he turned the trophy upside down and added, "It says, 'Made in Hong Kong.'"

Those Doggone Credits

Members of the Academy of Motion Picture Arts and Sciences nominated a dog for a screenwriting award—and didn't even know it.

It was all because writer Robert Towne was boiling mad at **Warner Brothers**.

Towne had labored eight years on the screenplay adaptation of *Greystroke: The Legend of Tarzan, Lord of the Apes*, which he hoped to direct. But Warner Brothers let Hugh Hudson direct the 1983 film instead. Adding insult to injury, Hudson brought in his own writer, Michael Austin, to polish up the script and share in the writing credit.

Towne, a highly respected Hollywood screenwriter, was so disgusted that in the film credits he replaced his name with that of P.H. Vazak—the name of his Hungarian sheepdog!

When the film was up for a screenwriting award, P.H. Vazak was one of the nominees announced at the Academy Awards. He didn't win, which was just as well. He was home, chewing on a bone.

Paging Geraldine!

Famed actress Geraldine Page was one of the most unprepared winners in Oscar history.

In 1985, Page received her eighth Academy Award nomination, this time for *The Trip To Bountiful*. She had never won before and didn't expect to win this time either. So at the ceremonies, she kicked off her shoes and stuck them under a seat.

When F. Murray Abraham dramatically announced the winner for Best Actress, he ripped open the envelope and gasped, "Oh, I consider this woman the greatest actress in the English language! Geraldine Page!"

Everyone in the audience leaped to their feet—except the winner. She was busy looking for her shoes!

After inelegantly fumbling with her pumps, the distinguished actress finally strode onstage where she gave a graceful acceptance speech.

"I wasn't prepared for this," Geraldine confessed later. "When I was searching for my shoes, my mind blew a fuse."